MW01681070

FROM DEATH TO HARVEST

Resurrection, First Fruits, and the Road to Shavuot

✦ ✦ ✦

The Prophetic Fulfillment of God's Appointed Times from the Cross to the Outpouring of the Spirit

Cheri B

Truths Coming Inc.
TruthsComing.com

From Death to Harvest

Resurrection, First Fruits, and the Road to Shavuot

ISBN (Print): 978-1-971522-03-6

ISBN (eBook): 978-1-971522-02-9

Published by Truths Coming Inc.
TruthsComing.com

Printed in the United States of America

Dedication

To the Lamb of God,

who was slain before the foundation of the world,

and to every hungry soul who is willing to dig

beneath the surface of tradition

to find the treasures God buried in His calendar.

He is risen.

He is the First Fruits.

And the harvest is still coming in.

Contents

Introduction: Why the Calendar Matters

I have learned over the years that God does not waste a single detail. He is not random. He is not approximate. When He set the sun and moon in the sky on the fourth day of creation, He was building a prophetic clock—one that would mark every major act of redemption in human history with precision.

This book is an invitation to walk with me through the most extraordinary season on God's calendar: the fifty days from Passover through Shavuot—what many know as Pentecost. This is not merely a historical survey or an academic exercise. This is a prophetic map. It is the story of how God declared the end from the beginning, embedding the death, burial, resurrection, and ascension of Yeshua (Jesus) and the outpouring of the Holy Spirit into the very fabric of His appointed times—His mo'adim.

> **Isaiah 46:10 —** *"Declaring the end from the beginning, and from ancient times things which have not been done, saying, 'My purpose will be established, and I will accomplish all My good pleasure.'"*

The Hebrew word **mo'ed** (plural **mo'adim**) means "appointed time" or "divine appointment." These are not merely Jewish holidays or cultural observances—they are rehearsals of redemption. Every year, the nation of Israel practiced what God was going to do. And when the time was full, Yeshua stepped onto the stage of history and fulfilled them—not approximately, not symbolically, but on the exact days, in the exact sequence, with surgical prophetic precision.

> **Leviticus 23:1-2 —** *"The LORD spoke again to Moses, saying, 'Speak to the sons of Israel and say to them, "The LORD's appointed times which you shall proclaim as holy convocations—My appointed times are these."'"*

Notice the language: these are "the LORD's appointed times." They do not belong to Israel alone. They belong to God. And He embedded them in the rhythm of creation so that all who have eyes to see would recognize His hand when He moved.

In this book, we will walk through five appointed times and the prophetic fulfillment embedded in each: Passover (Pesach), Unleavened Bread (Chag HaMatzot), First Fruits (Yom HaBikkurim), the Counting of the Omer, and the Feast of Weeks (Shavuot/Pentecost). Each one tells a chapter of the same story: the Lamb was slain, the bread of life went into the ground, the first fruits of the resurrection emerged, the harvest was counted, and the Spirit was poured out to empower the reapers.

This is the gospel written in the calendar. Let's read it together.

Chapter 1: Pesach — The Lamb Was Slain

The Original Passover

The story of Passover begins with a death sentence and a blood-bought deliverance. In Egypt, God's people were enslaved—brick-makers, oppressed, groaning under Pharaoh's hand. And God heard them.

> **Exodus 2:24–25 —** *"So God heard their groaning; and God remembered His covenant with Abraham, Isaac, and Jacob. God saw the sons of Israel, and God took notice of them."*

When it was time to deliver His people, God did not send an army. He sent a lamb.

> **Exodus 12:3, 5–7 —** *"Speak to all the congregation of Israel, saying, 'On the tenth of this month they are each one to take a lamb for themselves, according to their fathers' households, a lamb for each household.' ... 'Your lamb shall be an unblemished male a year old; you may take it from the sheep or from the goats. You shall keep it until the fourteenth day of the same month, then the whole assembly of the congregation of Israel is to kill it at twilight.*

> *Moreover, they shall take some of the blood and put it on the two doorposts and on the lintel of the houses in which they eat it.'"*

Here is the pattern: on the tenth of Nisan, the lamb was selected. For four days it lived among the family—inspected, examined, proven unblemished. On the fourteenth of Nisan, at twilight (**bein ha'arbayim**, literally "between the evenings"), the lamb was slaughtered and its blood was applied to the doorposts.

Then came the word that would echo through all of history:

> **Exodus 12:13 —** *"The blood shall be a sign for you on the houses where you live; and when I see the blood I will pass over you, and no plague will befall you to destroy you when I strike the land of Egypt."*

Yeshua: The Lamb of God

Every detail of the Passover lamb pointed to one Person. John the Baptist declared it openly:

> **John 1:29 —** *"The next day he saw Jesus coming to him and said, 'Behold, the Lamb of God who takes away the sin of the world!'"*

Consider the prophetic alignment. Yeshua entered Jerusalem on the tenth of Nisan—the exact day the Passover lamb was selected and brought into the household. For four days, He was examined and challenged by the Pharisees, the Sadducees, and the scribes. They found no fault in Him—just as the Passover lamb had to be found without blemish.

> **Luke 23:4 —** *"Then Pilate said to the chief priests and the crowds, 'I find no guilt in this man.'"*

> **1 Peter 1:18–19 —** *"...knowing that you were not redeemed with perishable things like silver or gold from your futile way of life inherited from your forefathers, but with precious blood, as of a lamb unblemished and spotless, the blood of Christ."*

On the fourteenth of Nisan—the very day and hour the Passover lambs were being slaughtered in the Temple—Yeshua breathed His last on the cross. Paul states it without ambiguity:

> **1 Corinthians 5:7 —** *"Clean out the old leaven so that you may be a new lump, just as you are in fact unleavened. For Christ our Passover also has been sacrificed."*

The blood of the lamb on the doorposts in Egypt was a shadow. The blood of Yeshua on the cross was the substance. In Egypt, the firstborn were spared. In Christ, all who apply His blood by faith are delivered from the power of sin and death—forever.

> **Isaiah 53:7 —** *"He was oppressed and He was afflicted, yet He did not open His mouth; like a lamb that is led to slaughter, and like a sheep that is silent before its shearers, so He did not open His mouth."*

The Prophetic Fulfillment in Detail

Let me lay it out plainly so you can see what God did:

Nisan 10 — The lamb is selected and brought into the household (Exodus 12:3). Yeshua enters Jerusalem on a donkey. The crowds cry "Hosanna!" He presents Himself as King and Lamb simultaneously (Matthew 21:1–11; Zechariah 9:9).

Nisan 10-13 — The lamb is inspected for blemishes (Exodus 12:5). Yeshua is questioned, tested, and challenged in the Temple by every faction of Jewish leadership. None can find fault

(Matthew 22:15–46; Mark 12:13–34; Luke 20:19–40).

Nisan 14 — The lamb is slaughtered at twilight (Exodus 12:6). Yeshua is crucified and dies at the ninth hour, approximately 3:00 PM—the very hour the Passover lambs are being offered in the Temple (Matthew 27:45–50; Mark 15:34–37).

The blood is applied — In Egypt, the blood goes on the doorposts and lintel (Exodus 12:7). On the cross, Yeshua's blood was shed at the place of the skull—Golgotha—and by faith, we apply it to the doorposts of our hearts (Romans 3:25; Ephesians 1:7).

✦ ✦ ✦

Not a single detail was accidental. The Passover lamb was not a metaphor. It was a prophecy in the form of a ritual, practiced for fourteen centuries until the day the True Lamb showed up and fulfilled it in His own body.

> **Hebrews 10:1 —** *"For the Law, since it has only a shadow of the good things to come and not the very form of things, can never, by the same sacrifices which they offer continually year by year, make perfect those who draw near."*

Chapter 2: Chag HaMatzot — The Sinless One in the Grave

The Feast of Unleavened Bread

Passover and Unleavened Bread are so closely linked that many people treat them as one feast. But Scripture distinguishes them. Passover falls on the fourteenth of Nisan. The Feast of Unleavened Bread begins on the fifteenth and runs for seven days.

> **Leviticus 23:5-6 —** *"In the first month, on the fourteenth day of the month at twilight is the LORD's Passover. Then on the fifteenth day of the same month there is the Feast of Unleavened Bread to the LORD; for seven days you shall eat unleavened bread."*

For seven days, all leaven was to be removed from the homes of Israel. Leaven in Scripture consistently symbolizes sin, corruption, and the permeating influence of evil. To eat unleavened bread was to declare: we are a people set apart. We have been delivered by blood and we walk in purity.

> **Exodus 12:15 —** *"Seven days you shall eat unleavened bread, but on the first day you shall remove leaven from your*

> *houses; for whoever eats anything leavened from the first day until the seventh day, that person shall be cut off from Israel."*

The Sinless Bread of Life

Yeshua is the unleavened bread. He is the One in whom there is no leaven—no sin, no corruption, no decay. He declared it Himself:

> **John 6:35 —** *"Jesus said to them, 'I am the bread of life; he who comes to Me will not hunger, and he who believes in Me will never thirst.'"*

The matzah used at Passover is pierced, striped, and without leaven. Isaiah prophesied it:

> **Isaiah 53:5 —** *"But He was pierced through for our transgressions, He was crushed for our iniquities; the chastening for our well-being fell upon Him, and by His scourging we are healed."*

On the fifteenth of Nisan—the first day of Unleavened Bread—Yeshua's body was in the tomb. The Sinless One was in the ground. The Bread of Life had been broken and buried. But here is the prophetic detail that matters: no corruption touched Him. Just as unleavened bread has no decay agent in it, Yeshua's body saw no decay in the grave.

> **Psalm 16:10 —** *"For You will not abandon my soul to Sheol; nor will You allow Your Holy One to undergo decay."*

> **Acts 2:27, 31 —** *"Because You will not abandon my soul to Hades, nor allow Your Holy One to undergo decay. ... he looked ahead and spoke of the resurrection of the Christ, that He was neither abandoned to Hades, nor did His flesh suffer decay."*

Peter quoted this Psalm on the day of Pentecost and applied it directly to the resurrection of Yeshua. David wrote the prophecy. Yeshua fulfilled it. Peter explained it. The Holy Spirit confirmed it.

The Burial of the Seed

There is a second layer here. When Yeshua was buried on the first day of Unleavened Bread, He was also fulfilling the agricultural parable He Himself had spoken:

> **John 12:24 —** *"Truly, truly, I say to you, unless a grain of wheat falls into the earth and dies, it remains alone; but if it dies, it bears much fruit."*

The grain must go into the ground. The seed must be buried. The bread must be broken. Without the burial, there is no harvest. This is not a tragedy—it is the divine pattern. Death is the prerequisite for resurrection, and burial is the prerequisite for the harvest.

> **2 Corinthians 5:21 —** *"He made Him who knew no sin to be sin on our behalf, so that we might become the righteousness of God in Him."*

The sinless bread was buried for sinful people. The unleavened One took our leaven upon Himself—not absorbing it, but destroying it—so that we could be presented before God as a new lump, clean and unleavened.

> **1 Corinthians 5:7-8 —** *"Clean out the old leaven so that you may be a new lump, just as you are in fact unleavened. For Christ our Passover also has been sacrificed. Therefore let us celebrate the feast, not with old leaven, nor with the leaven of malice and wickedness, but with the unleavened bread of sincerity and truth."*

✦ ✦ ✦

The Feast of Unleavened Bread is not over for us. We are still called to live unleavened lives—to walk in sincerity and truth, to remove the leaven of hypocrisy and malice from our houses and our hearts. The feast was a rehearsal. The Cross made it real. And our daily walk is the ongoing fulfillment.

Chapter 3: Yom HaBikkurim — The Resurrection of the First Fruits

The Feast of First Fruits

Of all the appointed times, First Fruits may be the most under-taught—and yet it contains one of the most precise prophetic fulfillments in all of Scripture.

> **Leviticus 23:10-11 —** *"Speak to the sons of Israel and say to them, 'When you enter the land which I am going to give to you and reap its harvest, then you shall bring in the sheaf of the first fruits of your harvest to the priest. He shall wave the sheaf before the LORD for you to be accepted; on the day after the sabbath the priest shall wave it.'"*

The Feast of First Fruits was observed on the day after the Sabbath during the Feast of Unleavened Bread. The priest would take the first sheaf of the barley harvest—the very first portion of the crop that came up from the ground—and wave it before the LORD as a declaration: the harvest is coming. This first portion guarantees the rest.

The waving of the sheaf was an act of faith. The farmer had not yet gathered the full harvest. But by offering the first fruits, he was declaring: because this came up, the rest will follow.

Yeshua: The First Fruits from the Dead

Paul makes the connection with absolute clarity:

> **1 Corinthians 15:20-23 —** *"But now Christ has been raised from the dead, the first fruits of those who are asleep. For since by a man came death, by a man also came the resurrection of the dead. For as in Adam all die, so also in Christ all will be made alive. But each in his own order: Christ the first fruits, after that those who are Christ's at His coming."*

Yeshua rose from the dead on the Feast of First Fruits—the exact day the priest would wave the first sheaf of the barley harvest before the LORD. The timing is not coincidental. It is prophetic. He is the first sheaf. He is the first portion of the resurrection harvest. And because He came up from the ground, we who belong to Him are guaranteed to follow.

Consider the imagery: the grain of wheat fell into the ground and died (John 12:24). It was buried during Unleavened Bread. And on the day of First Fruits, the first shoot broke through the soil. The tomb was empty. The sheaf was waved. The Father accepted the offering.

The Resurrection Morning

The Gospel accounts paint the picture:

> **Matthew 28:1-6 —** *"Now after the Sabbath, as it began to dawn toward the first day of the week, Mary Magdalene and the other Mary came to look at the grave. And behold, a severe earthquake had occurred, for an angel of the Lord descended from heaven and came and rolled away the stone and sat upon it. And his appearance was like lightning, and his clothing as white as snow. The guards shook for fear of him and became like dead men. The angel said to the women, 'Do not be afraid; for I know that you are looking for Jesus who has been crucified. He is not here, for He has risen, just as He said. Come, see the place where He was lying.'"*

He is not here. He has risen. Consider the weight of this: by the time the priest lifted the first sheaf of barley before the LORD in the Temple, Yeshua had already risen—having come forth from the grave after the Sabbath ended on Saturday evening. Whether He stood among them in the Temple courts unrecognized, or whether the Father raised Him at the very moment the priests were offering the first fruits, the prophetic alignment is breathtaking. He is the true First Fruits—presented before the Father and accepted.

A Harvest Guarantee

The theology of first fruits is the theology of guarantee. The first portion sanctifies the whole.

> **Romans 11:16 —** *"If the first piece of dough is holy, the lump is also; and if the root is holy, the branches are also."*

Because Yeshua rose, we will rise. His resurrection is not an isolated miracle—it is the down payment, the earnest, the guarantee of the full harvest to come. Every believer who has died in Christ is a seed in the ground, waiting for the harvest shout.

> **1 Thessalonians 4:14 —** *"For if we believe that Jesus died and rose again, even so God will bring with Him those who have fallen asleep in Jesus."*

> **Romans 8:11 —** *"But if the Spirit of Him who raised Jesus from the dead dwells in you, He who raised Christ*

> *Jesus from the dead will also give life to your mortal bodies through His Spirit who dwells in you."*

Matthew 27: The First Fruits Preview

There is a passage in Matthew that is often overlooked, but it may be one of the most stunning first fruits fulfillments in the Gospels:

> **Matthew 27:52–53 —** *"The tombs were opened, and many bodies of the saints who had fallen asleep were raised; and coming out of the tombs after His resurrection they entered the holy city and appeared to many."*

When Yeshua rose, He did not rise alone. Saints came out of their tombs and appeared in Jerusalem. This was the wave offering in action—the first fruits of the resurrection harvest, presented before the people as a testimony: the harvest has begun.

The priest waved one sheaf, but that sheaf represented an entire field. Yeshua is the first fruits, and these resurrected saints were part of the wave offering—a down payment on the full resurrection that is coming.

✦ ✦ ✦

Every Resurrection Sunday, whether we realize it or not, we are celebrating the Feast of First Fruits. The empty tomb is not just a historical event. It is a harvest announcement. The first sheaf has been waved. The field is ripe. And the Harvester is coming back for the rest.

Chapter 4: Sefirat HaOmer — Counting the Days Between Resurrection and Power

The Command to Count

Between First Fruits and Shavuot lies one of the most overlooked yet prophetically significant seasons on God's calendar: the Counting of the Omer. It is not a feast day itself, but a bridge—a season of anticipation, preparation, and growing expectation.

> **Leviticus 23:15-16 —** *"You shall also count for yourselves from the day after the sabbath, from the day when you brought in the sheaf of the wave offering; there shall be seven complete sabbaths. You shall count fifty days to the day after the seventh sabbath; then you shall present a new grain offering to the LORD."*

From the day the first fruits sheaf was waved, Israel was commanded to count forty-nine days—seven complete weeks—and on the fiftieth day, to present a new grain offering. This is the Omer count. It connects the barley harvest (First Fruits) to the wheat harvest (Shavuot). It is a season of growth, of maturation, of the grain moving from tender shoot to ripe head.

The Forty Days with the Risen Lord

Now consider what happened prophetically during this exact season. After His resurrection on the day of First Fruits, Yeshua did not immediately ascend. He remained on earth for forty days:

> **Acts 1:3 —** *"To these He also presented Himself alive after His suffering, by many convincing proofs, appearing to them over a period of forty days and speaking of the things concerning the kingdom of God."*

For forty days during the Omer count, the risen Yeshua walked among His disciples, teaching them, opening the Scriptures to them, showing them His hands and His side. This was not random. The Omer season is a season of preparation—and Yeshua was preparing His disciples for what was coming on day fifty.

Post-Resurrection Appearances

During these forty days, the Scriptures record multiple appearances of the risen Lord, each one strengthening, teaching, and commissioning:

> **Luke 24:27 —** *"Then beginning with Moses and with all the prophets, He*

explained to them the things concerning Himself in all the Scriptures."

Luke 24:44-45 — *"Now He said to them, 'These are My words which I spoke to you while I was still with you, that all things which are written about Me in the Law of Moses and the Prophets and the Psalms must be fulfilled.' Then He opened their minds to understand the Scriptures."*

John 20:19-22 — *"So when it was evening on that day, the first day of the week, and when the doors were shut where the disciples were, for fear of the Jews, Jesus came and stood in their midst and said to them, 'Peace be with you.' And when He had said this, He showed them both His hands and His side. The disciples then rejoiced when they saw the Lord. So Jesus said to them again, 'Peace be with you; as the Father has sent Me, I also send you.' And when He had said this, He breathed on them and said to them, 'Receive the Holy Spirit.'"*

John 21:15-17 — *"So when they had finished breakfast, Jesus said to Simon Peter, 'Simon, son of John, do you love Me more than these?' He said to Him, 'Yes, Lord; You know that I love You.' He*

> *said to him, 'Tend My lambs.' ... He said to him, 'Shepherd My sheep.' ... He said to him, 'Tend My sheep.'"*

During the Omer, the grain is maturing. And during these forty days, the disciples were maturing. They were being shaped from frightened followers into commissioned apostles. The season between resurrection and Pentecost was not dead space—it was growing season.

The Number Forty: God's Pattern of Preparation

Before we get to the Ascension, we need to stop and ask: why forty? Why not thirty days? Why not fifty? Because in Scripture, the number forty is never random. It is one of the most consistent patterns in the entire Bible, and it always signals the same thing: a period of testing, preparation, and transition before God does something new. Forty is the hallway between two rooms—the old season is over, the new one has not yet begun, and the forty is where you are proven and refined for what is coming.

Look at the thread that runs from Genesis to Acts:

The Flood — Rain fell for forty days and forty nights, washing away the old world before God established a new covenant with Noah (Genesis 7:12, 17).

> **Genesis 7:12 —** *"The rain fell upon the earth for forty days and forty nights."*

Moses on Sinai — Moses spent forty days on the mountain receiving the Torah before bringing God's instruction down to Israel. When the people failed with the golden calf, he went back up for another forty days to intercede (Exodus 24:18; 34:28).

> **Exodus 24:18 —** *"Moses entered the midst of the cloud as he went up to the mountain; and Moses was on the mountain forty days and forty nights."*

The Twelve Spies — The spies scouted the Promised Land for forty days. When Israel refused to trust God's report, He assigned forty years of wilderness wandering—one year for each day of unbelief (Numbers 13:25; 14:34).

> **Numbers 14:34 —** *"According to the number of days which you spied out the land, forty days, for every day you shall bear your guilt a year, even forty years, and you will know My opposition."*

Israel in the Wilderness — For forty years God tested and prepared His people before they entered the land of promise. Moses told them the purpose plainly (Deuteronomy 8:2).

> **Deuteronomy 8:2 —** *"You shall remember all the way which the LORD your God has led you in the wilderness these forty years, that He might humble you, testing you, to know what was in your heart, whether you would keep His commandments or not."*

Goliath's Challenge — The giant taunted Israel for forty days before David rose up and defeated him—a shepherd boy who had been prepared in obscurity for this moment (1 Samuel 17:16).

> **1 Samuel 17:16 —** *"The Philistine came forward morning and evening for forty days and took his stand."*

Elijah's Journey — After his confrontation on Carmel, Elijah traveled forty days and forty nights in the strength of one meal to reach Horeb—the mountain of God—where the LORD spoke to him in a still, small voice (1 Kings 19:8).

> **1 Kings 19:8 —** *"So he arose and ate and drank, and went in the strength of that food forty days and forty nights to Horeb, the mountain of God."*

Nineveh's Reprieve — God gave the city forty days to repent before judgment would fall. They repented, and God relented (Jonah 3:4).

> **Jonah 3:4 —** *"Then Jonah began to go through the city one day's walk; and he cried out and said, 'Yet forty days and Nineveh will be overthrown.'"*

Yeshua in the Wilderness — Before launching His public ministry, Yeshua was led by the Spirit into the wilderness for forty days of fasting and temptation. Where Israel failed their forty-year test, Yeshua passed His forty-day test—answering every temptation with the Word of God (Matthew 4:1–2; Luke 4:1–2).

> **Matthew 4:1-2 —** *"Then Jesus was led up by the Spirit into the wilderness to be tempted by the devil. And after He had fasted forty days and forty nights, He then became hungry."*

Yeshua After the Resurrection — And now, after conquering death itself, Yeshua spent forty days with His disciples before ascending—teaching, commissioning, and preparing them for the outpouring of the Spirit (Acts 1:3).

Do you see it? Forty is always the bridge. It is always preparation. The flood prepared the earth for a new beginning. Sinai prepared Israel for covenant life. The wilderness prepared a generation for the Promised Land. The desert prepared Yeshua for ministry. And the forty days after the resurrection prepared the disciples for Pentecost.

God does not skip the forty. He never rushes the preparation. Because what comes after the forty—the new covenant, the Promised Land, the ministry, the outpouring—requires people who have been tested and found ready. The forty is not a delay. It is the proving ground.

✦ ✦ ✦

The Ascension: Day Forty

On the fortieth day of the Omer, Yeshua ascended to the Father. He had completed His post resurrection ministry and now returned to the right hand of God:

> **Acts 1:9-11** — *"And after He had said these things, He was lifted up while they were looking on, and a cloud received Him out of their sight. And as they were gazing intently into the sky while He was going, behold, two men in white clothing stood beside them. They also said, 'Men of Galilee, why do you stand looking into the sky? This Jesus, who has been taken up from you into heaven, will*

> *come in just the same way as you have watched Him go into heaven.'"*

But before He left, He gave them a command:

> **Acts 1:4-5 —** *"Gathering them together, He commanded them not to leave Jerusalem, but to wait for what the Father had promised, 'Which,' He said, 'you heard of from Me; for John baptized with water, but you will be baptized with the Holy Spirit not many days from now.'"*

Wait. Stay in Jerusalem. Something is coming on the fiftieth day. The Omer count is not over yet. Ten more days remain. And what happens on day fifty will change everything.

The Ten Days of Prayer

Between the Ascension (day forty) and Shavuot (day fifty), the disciples did exactly what Yeshua commanded:

> **Acts 1:14 —** *"These all with one mind were continually devoting themselves to prayer, along with the women, and Mary the mother of Jesus, and with His brothers."*

For ten days, they prayed. They waited. They counted. They anticipated. The grain was almost ripe. The harvest was about to break open. And every one of those days was prophetically mapped on the calendar God had given to Moses more than fourteen hundred years earlier.

The Number Ten: Divine Order and Complete Testing

Just as the number forty marks preparation, the number ten in Scripture carries its own distinct weight. Ten represents **completeness of divine order**—the full measure required before God acts, the complete cycle of testing, and the minimum threshold of corporate authority. It is not accidental that the disciples waited exactly ten days between the Ascension and the outpouring. God was finishing a pattern He had been building since Genesis.

Look at how the number ten threads through the whole counsel of Scripture:

Ten Words of Creation — God spoke ten times in Genesis 1 ("And God said..."), bringing the entire created order into existence through ten divine utterances. The rabbis have long recognized this. Ten words framed the world (Genesis 1:3, 6, 9, 11, 14, 20, 24, 26, 28, 29).

Ten Generations from Adam to Noah — God counted ten generations of increasing wickedness before He brought the judgment of the flood. Ten was the full measure of patience before divine action (Genesis 5).

Ten Generations from Noah to Abraham — After the flood, God again counted ten generations before He called Abraham and launched His covenant plan. The number ten marked the completion of one era and the beginning of another (Genesis 11).

The Ten Plagues — God did not send one plague or five. He sent ten—a complete dismantling of Egypt's gods and Pharaoh's power. Each plague was targeted, and the tenth —the death of the firstborn—required the blood of the lamb. Ten plagues completed the judgment; then deliverance came (Exodus 7–12).

> **Exodus 7:4-5 —** *"When Pharaoh does not listen to you, then I will lay My hand on Egypt and bring out My hosts, My people the sons of Israel, from the land of Egypt by great judgments. The Egyptians shall know that I am the LORD, when I stretch out My hand on Egypt and bring out the sons of Israel from their midst."*

The Ten Commandments — God did not give nine commandments or twelve. He gave ten—the complete moral law, the foundation of covenant life, written by His own finger on two tablets of stone. Ten represents the complete standard of divine righteousness (Exodus 20:1–17; Deuteronomy 5:6–21).

> **Exodus 34:28 —** *"So he was there with the LORD forty days and forty nights; he did not eat bread or drink water. And He wrote on the tablets the words of the covenant, the Ten Commandments."*

Ten Spies and the Test of Faith — Twelve spies went into the land, but ten came back with a faithless report. It was the ten who swayed the congregation to rebellion. The number ten, representing completeness, here represented the complete failure of Israel's faith—and God's response was forty years in the wilderness (Numbers 13:25–33; 14:22–23).

> **Numbers 14:22-23 —** *"Surely all the men who have seen My glory and My signs which I performed in Egypt and in the wilderness, yet have put Me to the test these ten times and have not listened to My voice, shall by no means see the land which I swore to their fathers, nor shall any of those who spurned Me see it."*

Notice: God said Israel had tested Him **ten times**. Ten was the complete measure of testing. After ten, the verdict was rendered.

Ten Righteous in Sodom — When Abraham interceded for Sodom, God agreed to spare the entire city for the sake of ten righteous people. Ten was the minimum threshold—the quorum of righteousness required for corporate mercy. There were not ten, and judgment fell (Genesis 18:32).

> **Genesis 18:32 —** *"Then he said, 'Oh may the Lord not be angry, and I shall speak only this once; suppose ten are found there?' And He said, 'I will not destroy it on account of the ten.'"*

This is significant. In Jewish tradition, ten became the number required for a **minyan**—the minimum assembly for corporate worship and prayer. And in that upper room, there were far more than ten. The hundred and twenty who gathered in one accord exceeded the threshold many times over (Acts 1:15).

The Tenth Day of the First Month — On the tenth of Nisan, the Passover lamb was selected (Exodus 12:3). On the tenth of Tishri, the Day of Atonement was observed—the holiest day on the calendar, when the high priest entered the Holy of Holies (Leviticus 23:27). The tenth day marked the point of divine selection and the point of divine atonement.

> **Leviticus 23:27 —** *"On exactly the tenth day of this seventh month is the day of atonement; it shall be a holy convocation for you, and you shall humble your souls and present an offering by fire to the LORD."*

The Tithe: A Tenth — God required a tenth of the increase—the tithe. The tenth portion belonged to Him. It was the part that sanctified the whole. By giving the tenth, the remaining ninety was declared clean and blessed (Leviticus 27:30; Malachi 3:10).

> **Leviticus 27:30 —** *"Thus all the tithe of the land, of the seed of the land or of the fruit of the tree, is the LORD's; it is holy to the LORD."*

Daniel's Ten Days of Testing — When Daniel and his companions refused the king's food in Babylon, they proposed a test: ten days of vegetables and water. At the end of ten days, they were found healthier and stronger than all the rest. Ten days completed the test and vindicated their faithfulness (Daniel 1:12–15).

> **Daniel 1:12, 15 —** *"Please test your servants for ten days, and let us be given some vegetables to eat and water to drink. ... At the end of ten days their appearance seemed better and they were fatter than all the youths who had been eating the king's choice food."*

Ten Days of Tribulation in Revelation — To the church in Smyrna, Yeshua said they would face tribulation for ten days—a complete but limited period of testing before vindication (Revelation 2:10).

> **Revelation 2:10 —** *"Do not fear what you are about to suffer. Behold, the devil is about to cast some of you into prison, so that you will be tested, and you will have tribulation for ten days. Be faithful until death, and I will give you the crown of life."*

Do you see the pattern? Ten is always the full measure. Ten plagues completed the judgment on Egypt. Ten commandments completed the moral law. Ten times Israel tested God and the verdict was rendered. Ten righteous would have spared a city. Ten days completed Daniel's test. And ten days of prayer in the upper room completed the preparation for the outpouring of the Holy Spirit.

The disciples did not wait ten days because they were idle or because God was delayed. They waited ten days because the divine order required it. Just as the forty days of the Omer were the bridge of preparation, these final ten days were the threshold of completeness—the last measure of corporate unity, prayer, and surrender before heaven opened.

After the ten, God moved. The Spirit fell. And nothing was ever the same.

✦ ✦ ✦

The Counting of the Omer teaches us something the modern church desperately needs to relearn: there is a season between the promise and the power. Between the resurrection and the outpouring, there is counting—there is preparation—there is growing up. God does not skip steps. He numbers the days because every day matters.

Chapter 5: Shavuot — The Harvest and the Outpouring

The Feast of Weeks

Shavuot—the Feast of Weeks, known in the Greek world as Pentecost (meaning "fiftieth")—is the culmination of the Omer count. It is the fiftieth day. It is the wheat harvest. It is the day God chose to write His law on tablets of stone at Sinai—and the day He chose to write His law on human hearts by the Holy Spirit.

> **Leviticus 23:15-17 —** *"You shall also count for yourselves from the day after the sabbath, from the day when you brought in the sheaf of the wave offering; there shall be seven complete sabbaths. You shall count fifty days to the day after the seventh sabbath; then you shall present a new grain offering to the LORD. You shall bring in from your dwelling places two loaves of bread for a wave offering, made of two-tenths of an ephah; they shall be of fine flour, baked with leaven as first fruits to the LORD."*

Notice something critical: the two loaves at Shavuot were baked **with leaven**. This is the only feast where leavened bread is presented. At Passover and Unleavened Bread, all leaven is removed. But at Shavuot, leavened loaves are waved before the LORD. Why? Because these loaves represent the church—the redeemed harvest of believing Jews and Gentiles, people who still have sin in their nature but are accepted before God through the blood of the Lamb and the fire of the Spirit.

The Number Fifty: Jubilee, Liberty, and New Beginning

We have already seen that forty is the number of preparation and ten is the number of divine completeness. Fifty is what happens when preparation meets completeness: forty plus ten equals fifty. And in Scripture, the number fifty always carries the same thundering declaration —**liberty, release, and the inauguration of something entirely new**.

The foundation of this pattern is the Year of Jubilee:

> **Leviticus 25:10 —** *"You shall thus consecrate the fiftieth year and proclaim a release through the land to all its inhabitants. It shall be a jubilee for you, and each of you shall return to his own property, and each of you shall return to his family."*

Every fiftieth year, the economy of Israel was reset. Debts were canceled. Slaves were freed. Land that had been sold reverted to its original family. No matter how far you had fallen, no matter how much you had lost, the fiftieth year restored you to your inheritance. The Hebrew word for jubilee—**yovel**—is associated with the ram's horn, the shofar blast that announced freedom.

> **Leviticus 25:8-9 —** *"You are also to count off seven sabbaths of years for yourself, seven times seven years, so that you have the time of the seven sabbaths of years, namely, forty-nine years. You shall then sound a ram's horn abroad on the tenth day of the seventh month; on the day of atonement you shall sound a horn all through your land."*

Notice the structure: seven times seven—forty-nine—then the fiftieth. This is the exact pattern of the Omer count. Seven complete Sabbaths—forty-nine days—then the fiftieth day is Shavuot. The Feast of Weeks is built on the architecture of Jubilee. It is not a coincidence. It is a blueprint.

Now consider what Yeshua declared at the very start of His public ministry. Standing in the synagogue at Nazareth, He opened the scroll of Isaiah and read:

> **Luke 4:18–19 —** *"The Spirit of the Lord is upon Me, because He anointed Me to preach the gospel to the poor. He has sent Me to proclaim release to the captives, and recovery of sight to the blind, to set free those who are oppressed, to proclaim the favorable year of the Lord."*
>
> **Luke 4:21 —** *"And He began to say to them, 'Today this Scripture has been fulfilled in your hearing.'"*

The "favorable year of the Lord" is the Year of Jubilee. Yeshua was announcing that He Himself was the Jubilee—the living fulfillment of everything the fiftieth year pointed to. Release for captives. Sight for the blind. Freedom for the oppressed. Debts canceled. Inheritance restored.

And when did the Spirit fall to empower this Jubilee message to go to the nations? On the fiftieth day. On Shavuot. On Pentecost.

The parallels are layered and intentional:

Jubilee canceled debts. At Pentecost, Peter proclaimed the forgiveness of sins—the ultimate debt cancellation (Acts 2:38).

Jubilee freed slaves. At Pentecost, the Spirit set people free from bondage to sin and death. Paul would later write that where the Spirit of the Lord is, there is liberty (2 Corinthians 3:17).

Jubilee restored inheritance. At Pentecost, believers received the Holy Spirit as the down payment—the **arrabon**, the guarantee—of their eternal inheritance (Ephesians 1:13–14).

Jubilee was announced by a shofar blast. At Pentecost, there came a sound from heaven like a violent rushing wind—the divine shofar announcing that the age of the Spirit had begun (Acts 2:2).

> **Ephesians 1:13–14 —** *"In Him, you also, after listening to the message of truth, the gospel of your salvation—having also believed, you were sealed in Him with the Holy Spirit of promise, who is given as a pledge of our inheritance, with a view to the redemption of God's own possession, to the praise of His glory."*
>
> **2 Corinthians 3:17 —** *"Now the Lord is the Spirit, and where the Spirit of the Lord is, there is liberty."*

Fifty is the number of a new beginning that can never be undone. After the Jubilee, you are free

—not temporarily, but by divine decree. After Pentecost, the Spirit was poured out—not for a season, but permanently. The fiftieth day did not just mark a moment in time. It inaugurated an entirely new era: the age of the Spirit, the age of the harvest, the age of liberty.

This is why God chose the fiftieth day. Not the forty-fifth. Not the sixtieth. The fiftieth—because the fiftieth is Jubilee. And Jubilee means everything that was lost is coming back.

✦ ✦ ✦

Sinai: The First Shavuot

Jewish tradition holds that the giving of the Torah at Mount Sinai occurred on Shavuot—fifty days after the Exodus from Egypt. The parallels are extraordinary:

> **Exodus 19:16-18 —** *"So it came about on the third day, when it was morning, that there were thunder and lightning flashes and a thick cloud upon the mountain and a very loud trumpet sound, so that all the people who were in the camp trembled. And Moses brought the people out of the camp to meet God, and they stood at the foot of the mountain. Now Mount Sinai was all in smoke because the LORD descended*

> *upon it in fire; and its smoke ascended like the smoke of a furnace, and the whole mountain quaked violently."*

At Sinai, God descended in fire. He spoke in a voice that shook the mountain. He gave His Torah—His instruction—written on stone tablets by His own finger. And the people stood at a distance, trembling.

But God promised through the prophets that a day was coming when the Torah would not be written on stone but on flesh:

> **Jeremiah 31:33 —** *"'But this is the covenant which I will make with the house of Israel after those days,' declares the LORD, 'I will put My law within them and on their heart I will write it; and I will be their God, and they shall be My people.'"*

> **Ezekiel 36:26–27 —** *"Moreover, I will give you a new heart and put a new spirit within you; and I will remove the heart of stone from your flesh and give you a heart of flesh. I will put My Spirit within you and cause you to walk in My statutes, and you will be careful to observe My ordinances."*

Pentecost: The Fulfillment

On the fiftieth day after the resurrection—on the Feast of Shavuot—the Father kept His promise:

> **Acts 2:1-4 —** *"When the day of Pentecost had fully come, they were all together in one place. And suddenly there came from heaven a noise like a violent rushing wind, and it filled the whole house where they were sitting. And there appeared to them tongues as of fire distributing themselves, and they rested on each one of them. And they were all filled with the Holy Spirit and began to speak with other tongues, as the Spirit was giving them utterance."*

Look at the parallels between Sinai and Pentecost. At Sinai: fire came down on the mountain. At Pentecost: tongues of fire came down on each person. At Sinai: God spoke in a voice all nations could hear. At Pentecost: the disciples spoke in the languages of all nations. At Sinai: the law was written on stone. At Pentecost: the law was written on hearts. At Sinai: three thousand people died for the golden calf (Exodus 32:28). At Pentecost: three thousand people were saved (Acts 2:41).

The letter kills, but the Spirit gives life (2 Corinthians 3:6). The contrast could not be sharper.

Peter's Sermon: The Prophets Fulfilled

When the crowd gathered in amazement and confusion, Peter stood and declared that this was the fulfillment of what Joel had prophesied:

> **Acts 2:16-21 —** *"...but this is what was spoken of through the prophet Joel: 'And it shall be in the last days,' God says, 'that I will pour forth of My Spirit on all mankind; and your sons and your daughters shall prophesy, and your young men shall see visions, and your old men shall dream dreams; even on My bondslaves, both men and women, I will in those days pour forth of My Spirit and they shall prophesy. And I will grant wonders in the sky above and signs on the earth below, blood, and fire, and vapor of smoke. The sun will be turned into darkness and the moon into blood, before the great and glorious day of the Lord shall come. And it shall be that everyone who calls on the name of the Lord will be saved.'"*

Peter then connected the dots all the way back through the appointed times:

> **Acts 2:22-24 —** *"Men of Israel, listen to these words: Jesus the Nazarene, a man attested to you by God with miracles and wonders and signs which God performed through Him in your midst, just as you yourselves know—this Man, delivered over by the predetermined plan and foreknowledge of God, you nailed to a cross by the hands of godless men and put Him to death. But God raised Him up again, putting an end to the agony of death, since it was impossible for Him to be held in its power."*

There it is. The full arc. Passover: He was delivered and crucified. Unleavened Bread: He was buried. First Fruits: God raised Him up. And now at Shavuot: the Spirit is poured out as the evidence that He has ascended to the right hand of the Father and received the promise.

> **Acts 2:32-33 —** *"This Jesus God raised up again, to which we are all witnesses. Therefore having been exalted to the right hand of God, and having received from the Father the promise of the Holy Spirit, He has poured forth this which you both see and hear."*

The Two Loaves and the Harvest

Remember the two leavened loaves waved at Shavuot? On the day of Pentecost, two groups were gathered into one: Jews and eventually Gentiles, brought together as one body, one new humanity, presented before the Father through the Spirit.

> **Ephesians 2:14–16 —** *"For He Himself is our peace, who made both groups into one and broke down the barrier of the dividing wall, by abolishing in His flesh the enmity, which is the Law of commandments contained in ordinances, so that in Himself He might make the two into one new man, thus establishing peace, and might reconcile them both in one body to God through the cross, by it having put to death the enmity."*

The harvest came in. Three thousand souls on that first day—the first fruits of the church's wheat harvest. And the harvest has been coming in ever since.

> **Acts 2:41 —** *"So then, those who had received his word were baptized; and that day there were added about three thousand souls."*

✦ ✦ ✦

Shavuot is not merely a historical event. It is the ongoing reality of the Spirit's work. The same Spirit who descended on that fiftieth day is still writing God's law on hearts. The same fire that sat on the heads of the hundred and twenty is still available to every believer who will wait, pray, and count the cost.

Chapter 6: The Prophetic Thread — Seeing the Whole Tapestry

One Story, One Calendar, One God

Now that we have walked through each appointed time individually, I want to step back and help you see the full picture. Because what God did across these fifty days is not a collection of disconnected miracles. It is one continuous narrative, written into the agricultural and liturgical calendar of Israel, fulfilled by one Man in one season, confirmed by one Spirit.

Let me lay it out as a single prophetic timeline:

Nisan 10 — Lamb Selection Day: Yeshua enters Jerusalem. He is the Lamb selected and presented to the nation (Exodus 12:3; Matthew 21:1–11).

Nisan 10–13 — Inspection Days: Yeshua is examined by every faction—Pharisees, Sadducees, Herodians, scribes—and no fault is found (Exodus 12:5; Matthew 22–23; Luke 20; John 18:38).

Nisan 14 — Passover (Pesach): Yeshua is crucified at the exact hour the Passover lambs are slain in the Temple (Exodus 12:6; 1 Corinthians 5:7; Matthew 27:45–50).

Nisan 15 — Unleavened Bread (Chag HaMatzot): Yeshua's sinless body rests in the tomb. No corruption touches Him (Leviticus 23:6; Psalm 16:10; Acts 2:27).

Nisan 17 — First Fruits (Yom HaBikkurim): Yeshua rises from the dead—the first fruits of the resurrection harvest (Leviticus 23:10–11; 1 Corinthians 15:20–23).

Days 1-40 — Omer Count: Yeshua appears to His disciples over forty days, teaching them about the kingdom (Acts 1:3; Luke 24:27, 44–45).

Day 40 — Ascension: Yeshua ascends to the right hand of the Father (Acts 1:9–11).

Days 40-49 — Prayer and Waiting: The disciples pray in one accord, awaiting the promise (Acts 1:14).

Day 50 — Shavuot (Pentecost): The Holy Spirit falls. Tongues of fire. Languages of the nations. Three thousand souls harvested (Leviticus 23:15–17; Acts 2:1–4, 41; Joel 2:28-32).

The Agricultural Progression

God chose an agricultural society to carry His prophetic calendar, and the progression of the harvest tells the story:

Barley is the first crop to ripen in Israel. It is hardy, grows in rough conditions, and does not require ideal circumstances. Barley represents the resurrection—the first fruits that break through the soil even in the harshest conditions. Death could not hold Yeshua, just as barley pushes up through rocky ground.

Wheat is the later harvest—larger, more valuable, gathered with greater effort. Wheat represents the church, the broader harvest of souls that comes after the first fruits. The wheat harvest is gathered at Shavuot, and it continues to this day.

> **Matthew 9:37-38 —** *"Then He said to His disciples, 'The harvest is plentiful, but the workers are few. Therefore beseech the Lord of the harvest to send out workers into His harvest.'"*

The New Covenant Written in the Calendar

What we are seeing is that the New Covenant is not a break from the Old Testament. It is the fulfillment of it. The appointed times were always pointing to Yeshua. They were not made obsolete by His coming—they were completed.

> **Matthew 5:17-18 —** *"Do not think that I came to abolish the Law or the Prophets; I did not come to abolish but to fulfill. For truly I say to you, until heaven and earth pass away, not the smallest letter or stroke shall pass from the Law until all is accomplished."*
>
> **Colossians 2:16-17 —** *"Therefore no one is to act as your judge in regard to food or drink or in respect to a festival or a new moon or a Sabbath day—things which are a mere shadow of what is to come; but the substance belongs to Christ."*

The shadows belong to the calendar. The substance belongs to Christ. But the shadows still teach us, because they show us the shape of what cast them. When you understand the appointed times, you understand the gospel at a depth that most believers never reach.

What About the Fall Feasts?

This book covers the spring feasts—the feasts that have been fulfilled in Yeshua's first coming. But the calendar does not end at Shavuot. Three more appointed times await in the fall: the Feast of Trumpets (Yom Teruah), the Day of Atonement (Yom Kippur), and the Feast of Tabernacles (Sukkot).

These three feasts have not yet been fulfilled. They point to Yeshua's second coming: the trumpet blast, the final atonement, and God dwelling with His people forever. If the spring feasts were fulfilled to the exact day, we have every reason to believe the fall feasts will be as well.

> **Revelation 21:3 —** *"And I heard a loud voice from the throne, saying, 'Behold, the tabernacle of God is among men, and He will dwell among them, and they shall be His people, and God Himself will be among them.'"*

The calendar is not finished. The clock is still ticking. And the God who kept His appointments in the spring will keep them in the fall.

Chapter 7: Living in the Harvest — What This Means for Us Today

We Are Living Between the Feasts

If you have been following the prophetic calendar, you know where we stand. The spring feasts have been fulfilled. The fall feasts await fulfillment. That means we are living in the harvest season—the long summer between Shavuot and the Feast of Trumpets.

This is not a season of passivity. It is a season of labor. The Spirit has been poured out. The commission has been given. The harvest is ripe. And the Lord of the harvest is watching to see who will go into the field.

> **John 4:35 —** *"Do you not say, 'There are yet four months, and then comes the harvest'? Behold, I say to you, lift up your eyes and look on the fields, that they are white for harvest."*

The Power of the Spirit for the Harvest

Shavuot was never meant to be a one-time event. The Spirit was poured out to empower the church for the harvest—not for a single generation, but for every generation until Yeshua returns.

> **Acts 1:8 —** *"...but you will receive power when the Holy Spirit has come upon you; and you shall be My witnesses both in Jerusalem, and in all Judea and Samaria, and even to the remotest part of the earth."*

> **Acts 2:38-39 —** *"Peter said to them, 'Repent, and each of you be baptized in the name of Jesus Christ for the forgiveness of your sins; and you will receive the gift of the Holy Spirit. For the promise is for you and your children and for all who are far off, as many as the Lord our God will call to Himself.'"*

The promise is for you. The same Spirit. The same fire. The same power. Peter said the promise extends to all who are far off—that includes us, right here, right now, in this generation.

Counting Our Own Days

The Omer teaches us to count our days—to be intentional about the season of preparation between God's promises and their fulfillment. Not every day is a day of dramatic breakthrough. Some days are growing days. Some are waiting days. Some are days when the grain is maturing beneath the surface and nothing seems to be happening.

> **Psalm 90:12 —** *"So teach us to number our days, that we may present to You a heart of wisdom."*

Every day in the Omer mattered. Every day between the resurrection and Pentecost served a purpose. And every day of your life between the promise and the fulfillment has a purpose too. God does not waste a single sunrise.

A Call to the Harvest

I want to close this book the way Peter closed his Pentecost sermon—with a call to respond. The blood of the Lamb has been shed. The Bread of Life has been broken. The First Fruits have risen. The Spirit has been poured out. The harvest is in full swing.

The question is: where are you in the story?

Have you come under the blood of the Lamb? Have you let the leaven be purged from your life? Have you experienced the resurrection power of the risen Yeshua? Are you walking in the Spirit? Are you laboring in the harvest?

> **2 Corinthians 6:2 —** *"...for He says, 'At the acceptable time I listened to you, and on the day of salvation I helped you.' Behold, now is 'the acceptable time,' behold, now is 'the day of salvation.'"*

The appointed times were not ancient curiosities. They are the framework of God's redemptive plan—a plan that includes you. The calendar says so. The Cross proves it. The empty tomb guarantees it. And the Spirit empowers it.

✦ ✦ ✦

From death to harvest. From the blood on the doorpost to the fire on the head. From Pesach to Shavuot. It is one story, told by one God, fulfilled by one Savior, and carried forward by one Spirit in the hearts of every believer who will say yes.

He is risen. The first fruits have been waved. The harvest is here.

Let's get to work.

Appendix A: Complete Scripture Index

All Scripture quotations are from the New American Standard Bible (NASB), 1995 edition.

Genesis: 5 (ten generations); 7:12; 11 (ten generations); 18:32

Exodus: 2:24–25; 7:4–5; 12:3; 12:5–7; 12:6; 12:7; 12:13; 12:15; 19:16–18; 20:1–17; 24:18; 32:28; 34:28

Leviticus: 23:1–2; 23:5–6; 23:10–11; 23:15–16; 23:15–17; 23:27; 25:8–9; 25:10; 27:30

Numbers: 13:25; 13:25–33; 14:22–23; 14:34

Deuteronomy: 5:6–21; 8:2

1 Samuel: 17:16

1 Kings: 19:8

Psalm: 16:10; 90:12

Isaiah: 46:10; 53:5; 53:7

Jeremiah: 31:33

Ezekiel: 36:26–27

Daniel: 1:12, 15

Joel: 2:28–32

Jonah: 3:4

Zechariah: 9:9

Malachi: 3:10

Matthew: 4:1–2; 5:17–18; 9:37–38; 21:1–11; 22:15-46; 27:45–50; 27:52–53; 28:1–6

Mark: 12:13–34; 15:34–37

Luke: 4:1–2; 4:18–19; 4:21; 20:19–40; 23:4; 24:27; 24:44–45

John: 1:29; 4:35; 6:35; 12:24; 18:38; 20:19–22; 21:15–17

Acts: 1:3; 1:4–5; 1:8; 1:9–11; 1:14; 2:1–4; 2:16-21; 2:22–24; 2:27; 2:31; 2:32–33; 2:38–39; 2:41

Romans: 3:25; 8:11; 11:16

1 Corinthians: 5:7; 5:7–8; 15:20–23

2 Corinthians: 3:6; 3:17; 5:21; 6:2

Ephesians: 1:7; 1:13–14; 2:14–16

Colossians: 2:16–17

1 Thessalonians: 4:14

Hebrews: 10:1

1 Peter: 1:18–19

Revelation: 2:10; 21:3

Appendix B: The Spring Feasts — Prophecy and Fulfillment at a Glance

Feast	Hebrew Date	Prophetic Shadow	Fulfillment in Yeshua	Key Scripture
Passover (Pesach)	Nisan 14	Lamb slain; blood applied to doorposts	Yeshua crucified at the hour of sacrifice	1 Cor. 5:7; John 1:29
Unleavened Bread	Nisan 15–21	Leaven removed; pure bread eaten for seven days	Yeshua's sinless body buried; no decay touched Him	Psalm 16:10; Acts 2:27
First Fruits	Day after Sabbath during UB	First sheaf of barley waved before the LORD	Yeshua rises from the dead; first fruits of resurrection	1 Cor. 15:20–23; Matt. 28:1–6
Counting the Omer	49 days from First Fruits	Grain matures from barley to wheat	Yeshua appears for 40 days; disciples prepared	Acts 1:3; Luke 24:27
Shavuot (Pentecost)	Day 50 (Sivan 6)	Wheat harvest; two leavened loaves waved	Holy Spirit poured out; 3,000 saved; Torah on hearts	Acts 2:1–4, 41; Jer. 31:33

About the Author

Cheri B is a theologian, minister, author, songwriter, and recording artist whose creative and professional work is deeply rooted in her Christian faith. She holds a Master of Divinity in Pastoral Theology and brings a passion for Hebrew language, biblical scholarship, and prophetic ministry to everything she does.

As the founder of Truths Coming Inc. (TruthsComing.com), Cheri teaches and equips believers to dig beneath the surface of tradition and discover the treasures God has buried in His Word. She is also a recording artist releasing worship music under the name Cheri B through her label Remnant Recordings.

Cheri builds in both the natural and the spiritual—construction, ministry, music, books, and teachings. Her work reflects a conviction that God does not separate the sacred from the everyday, and that every act of building, creating, and stewarding can be an act of worship.

CheriB.me
TruthsComing.com

Remnant Recordings

Made in the USA
Coppell, TX
08 June 2026

79202041R00042